SPIRIT OF PLACE
LONDON

London, thou art the flower of cities all.

WILLIAM DUNBAR, 'TO THE CITY OF LONDON', c1501

Arcade Publishing · New York

Little, Brown and Company

ST PAUL'S CATHEDRAL

St Paul's should, I think, be loved from a distance; an interview should not be courted. The triumph of St Paul's is that, vast and serene, it broods protectively over the greatest city in the world, and is worthy of its office. The dome is magnificent: there is nothing finer: and that to me is St Paul's – a mighty mothering dome; not cold aisles and monstrous groups of statuary, not a whispering gallery and worried mosaics, not Americans with red guide books and typists eating their lunch. All that I want to forget.

St Paul's best appeal, true appeal, is external. It has no religious significance to me: it is the artistic culmination of London city, it is the symbol of London. And as such it is always thrilling. One of the best near views is from the footbridge from Charing Cross to Waterloo; one of the best distant views is from Parliament Hill. By no effort of imagination can one think of London without it.

E. V. LUCAS, *A WANDERER IN LONDON*, 1906

TOWER BRIDGE

The bridge is not ancient. It is exuberantly Victorian . . . a masterpiece of engineering. The giant bascules of the bridge weigh 1,000 tons, which can be raised to let a ship pass in a minute and a half. This occurs more than a dozen times a day and has indeed occurred about 325,000 times, without a single failure, since the contraption was built.

In some moods one feels the whole thing is some owlish and baronial fake from a German barony; in others, it has that unhappy familiar ugliness for which we begin to have an affectionate pity, reflecting that it has what in his literary way really the Londoner likes most: character. . . Seen in the kindness of fog or mist, the Tower Bridge has the beauty of a heavy web hung from the sky or floating like some ghostly schooner just above the surface of the water.

V. S. PRITCHETT, *LONDON PERCEIVED*, 1962

THE LIVELY CITY

I have passed all my days in London, until I have formed as many and intense local attachments as any of you mountaineers can have done with dead Nature. The lighted shops of the Strand and Fleet Street; the innumerable trades, tradesmen and customers, coaches, waggons, play houses; all the bustle and wickedness round about Covent Garden; the watchmen, drunken scenes, rattles; life awake, if you awake at all hours of the night; the impossibility of being dull in Fleet Street; the crowds, the very dirt and mud, the sun shining upon houses and pavements, the print-shops, the old book-stalls, parsons cheapening books, coffee-houses, steams of soup from kitchens, the pantomimes – London itself a pantomime and masquerade – all these things work themselves into my mind, and feed me, without a power of satiating me. The wonder of these sights impels me into night-walks about her crowded streets, and I often shed tears in the motley Strand from fullness of joy at so much life.

CHARLES LAMB, LETTER TO WILLIAM WORDSWORTH

COVENT GARDEN

The market itself presents a beautiful scene. In the clear morning air of an autumn day the whole of the vast square is distinctly seen from one end to the other. The sky is red and golden with the newly-risen sun, and the rays falling on the fresh and vivid colours of the fruit and vegetables, brightens up the picture as with a coat of varnish. There is no shouting, as at other markets, but a low murmuring hum is heard, like the sound of the sea at a distance, and through each entrance to the market the crowd sweeps by. Under the dark Piazza little bright dots of gas-lights are seen burning in the shops; and in the paved square the people pass and cross each other in all directions, hampers clash together, and excepting the carters from the country, every one is on the move. Cabbages are piled up into stacks as it were. Carts are heaped high with turnips, and bunches of carrots like huge red fingers are seen in all directions. Flower-girls, with huge bunches of violets under their arms, run past, leaving a trail of perfume behind them.

HENRY MAYHEW, *LONDON LABOUR AND THE LONDON POOR*, 1861

TRAFALGAR SQUARE

Of Trafalgar Square London has every right to be proud. Here at any rate, one feels, is a genuinely national attempt at a grandiose effect. The National Gallery façade is satisfactory in its British plainness and seriousness; St Martin's Church, with its whiteness emerging from its grime, is pure London; the houses on the east and west sides of the square are commendably rectangular and sturdy; the lions (although occupied only in guarding policemen's waterproofs) are imposing and very British: while the Nelson column is as tall and as commanding as any people, however artistic or passionately patriotic, could have made it. It is right. I am not sure but it touches sublimity. Apart, I mean altogether from the crowning figure and all that he stands for in personal valour, melancholy and charm, and all that he symbolizes: conquest itself – more than conquest, deliverance. Indeed with the idea of Nelson added, there is no question at all of sublimity; it is absolute.

E. V. LUCAS, *A WANDERER IN LONDON*, 1906

ST MARTIN-IN-THE-FIELDS

Trafalgar Square is so intimately associated with the everyday life of the metropolis that it seems difficult to realize that this fine open space, designed between 1829 and 1841 as a kind of War Memorial to the Nelson victories, is little more than a century old, and is some ten years younger than Piccadilly Circus. It was laid out on the site of the King's Mews, erected in 1732 and once the royal stables, together with a slum area which surrounded St Martin's Church, known as the Bermuda and Caribee Islands and Porridge Island, famous for its cook-shops . . . St Martin's Church, overlooking the north-east corner of Trafalgar Square, replaced an earlier edifice and is noteworthy on account of its handsome portico and lofty spire. It was begun in 1721 and completed in 1726, when George I gave 100 guineas to the workmen in addition to £29,000 which he contributed towards the cost of the building and to the organ. The entire cost was nearly £70,000.

HAROLD P. CLUNN, *THE FACE OF LONDON*, 1932

THE HEART OF WESTMINSTER

At Westminster, the river changes. The long doctoral façade of the innumerable, pricking spires and turrets of the Palace of Westminster; Big Ben's brown, enormous tower under its imperial pagoda, London's grandfather clock; close to them the Abbey, higher within than any other cathedral in England but dwarfed to outside view because one never gets more than half a sight of it; the school, tacked on to its cloisters, where Ben Jonson, Wren, Dryden, Cowper, and Gibbon were taught – these are a climax. Here London rules. At the sight, pride goes like a gong in the sentimental London heart. This, one realizes, is the place where Time itself is British, as British as Boadicea. Melodious in this deception, Big Ben utters the quarters and the hours in a grave voice that, at night, spreads over the city.

V. S. PRITCHETT, *LONDON PERCEIVED*, 1962

BUCKINGHAM PALACE

I'm Burlington Bertie
I rise at ten thirty
Then Buckingham Palace I view.
I stand in the Yard
While they're changing the Guard
And the King shouts across 'Toodle oo'.
The Prince of Wales' brother, along with some other,
Slaps me on the back, and says, 'Come round and see Mother.'
I'm Bert, Bert, and Royalty's hurt
When they ask me to dine, I say 'No'!
'I've just had a banana with Lady Diana
'I'm Burlington Bertie from Bow!'

WILLIAM HARGREAVES, 'BURLINGTON BERTIE FROM BOW', 1915

TROOPING THE COLOUR

The day's pageantry begins and ends at Buckingham Palace. His Majesty rides out from the forecourt and salutes the waiting crowd, who give him a special cheer on this, his official birthday. His procession along the Mall is headed by the band of the Household Cavalry, who also provide the Sovereign's escort. As the imposing cavalcade turns into the Horse Guards Parade, your eyes are attracted by the bands, drums and fifes of the Brigade of Guards, massed at the far end of the parade ground, a gorgeous, glittering company, but outshone by the five drum-majors in their state gold coats. The King's Colour is facing the bands, the Field Officer in Brigade-Waiting, who commands the parade, moves forward to greet the King, and the crowd cheer and wave handkerchiefs as the stately procession moves to its appointed place. The King, surrounded by a brilliant escort of high-ranking officers, takes up his position for the Royal Salute, inspects the line, and then watches the massed bands, marching and counter-marching, first in slow time, then breaking into quick time. The climax is reached when, with superb precision, a young Guards officer, attended by an escort, slowly, and with high dignity, troops the Colour down the line of Guards.

REX ALSTON IN *FLOWER OF CITIES*, 1949

18

Window Shopping

First one passes a watchmaker's, then a silk or fan store, now a silversmith's, a china or glass shop. The spirit booths are particularly tempting, for the English are in any case fond of strong drink. Here crystal flasks of every shape and form are exhibited: each one has a light behind it which makes all the different coloured spirits sparkle. Just as alluring are the confectioners and fruiterers, where, behind the handsome glass windows, pyramids of pineapples, figs, grapes, oranges and all manner of fruits are on show. Most of all we admired a stall with Argand and other lamps, situated in a corner-house, and forming a really dazzling spectacle; every variety of lamp, crystal, lacquer, and metal ones; silver and brass in every possible shade; large and small lamps . . .

Up to eleven o'clock at night there are as many people along this street as at Frankfurt during the fair, not to mention the eternal stream of coaches. The arrangement of the shops . . . with their adjoining living rooms, makes a very pleasant sight. For right through the excellently illuminated shop one can see many a charming family scene enacted.

SOPHIE V. LA ROCHE, *SOPHIE IN LONDON*, 1786

LONDON AT NIGHT

London at night
    With the gas lamps alight
Is renowned for its moral fragility
From ornate, sedate Pall Mall
To the dark romance of Regent's Canal.
Girls in large hats
Outside Boodle's and Pratt's
Lie in wait for the younger nobility
And they frequently compel
Some inebriated swell
To hop into a hansom
And shout through the transom,
'Drive home – drive home like hell!'
Men who survive
Piccadilly alive
And can take the air
In Leicester Square
And not be put to flight
Earnestly say
That Port Said and Bombay
Are a great deal more prim and upright
Than London at Night.

Noël Coward, from After the Ball, 1954

LONDON SEASONS

Gleaming with sunlight, each soft lawn
Lies fragrant beneath dew of dawn;
The spires and towers rise, far withdrawn,
    Through golden mist:
At sunset, linger beside Thames:
See now, what radiant lights and flames!
That ruby burns: that purple shames
    The amethyst.

Winter was long, and dark, and cold:
Chill rains! Grim fogs, black fold on fold,
Round street, and square, and river rolled!
    Ah, let it be:
Winter is gone! Soon comes July,
With wafts from hayfields by-and-by:
While in the dingiest courts you spy
    Flowers fair to see.

Take heart of grace: and let each hour
Break gently into bloom and flower:
Winter and sorrow have no power
    To blight all bloom.
One day, perchance, the sun will see
London's entire felicity:
And all her loyal children be
    Clear of all gloom.

A dream? Dreams often dreamed come true:
Our world would seem a world made new
To those, beneath the churchyard yew
    Laid long ago!
When we beneath like shadows bide,
Fair London, throned upon Thames' side,
May be our children's children's pride:
    And we shall know.

LIONEL JOHNSON, *LONDON TOWN*, 1915

In St James's Park

I want to say one other word about romantic London before we really enter Park Lane. Beneath one of her mists or light fogs London can become the most mysterious and beautiful city in the world. I know of nothing more bewitchingly lovely than the Serpentine on a still misty evening – when it is an unruffled lake of dim pearl-grey liquid, such stuff as sleep is made of. St James's Park at dusk on a winter's afternoon, seen from the suspension bridge, with all the lights of the Government offices reflected in its water, has less mystery but more romance. It might be the lake before an enchanted castle.

E. V. LUCAS, *A WANDERER IN LONDON*, 1906

THE ALBERT HALL

The Albert Hall was compared by Queen Victoria to the British Constitution, that flexible but solid entity that is such a mystery to foreigners. The Albert Hall is not at all mysterious; it stands on Kensington Gore like an enclosed Colosseum of red brick and terracotta with a glass and iron roof . . . The Hall's glowing red exterior, recently cleaned, is crowned by a frieze of figures enacting the arts and sciences and a celebratory inscription explaining that the building was erected 'in fulfilment of the intention of Albert Prince Consort', as indeed it was . . . The vast interior, like the St Pancras train shed, must be experienced to be believed. It seats thousands in tiers of boxes and upper seats circling an arena of standing or sometimes reclining 'promenaders' (in the summer anyway), and above all is the arcaded gallery with more 'promenaders' as in a painting by Veronese.

PRISCILLA METCALF, *VICTORIAN LONDON*, 1972

LONDON IS A FINE TOWN

O London is a dainty place,
  A great and gallant city!
For all the Streets are pav'd with gold,
  And all the folks are witty,
And there's your lords and ladies fine,
  That ride in coach and six;
That nothing drink but claret wine,
  And talk of politicks.

And there's your dames with dainty frames,
  With skins as white as milk;
Dressed every day in garments gay,
  Of satin and of silk.
And if your mind be so inclined
  To offer them your arm,
Pull out a handsome purse of gold,
  They can't resist the charm.

EIGHTEENTH-CENTURY STREET BALLAD

CRICKET AT LORD'S

Lord's! What tender recollections
   Does that famous name suggest!
What a crowd of fond reflections
   Throng my antiquated breast,
As I lounge in the Pavilion
   And, from my exalted seat,
Watch the undistinguished million
   Surging at my feet!

Hither, with a 'Rover's Ticket',
   In the days of youth I came;
Glued my eye upon the wicket,
   Missed no moment of the game,
While to feminine relations
   Whom I happened to escort
I explained the complications
   Of this form of sport!

Here, like ocean breakers roaring,
   I would stamp my feet and yell,
When I watched my heroes scoring,
   Or opponents' wickets fell;
Here, when inningses were ended,
   To the tents I turned my gaze,
Where the hock-cup subtly blended
   With the mayonnaise!

Happy days! Like shadows flitting
   O'er my mind, those mem'ries pass!
Now, in the Pavilion sitting,
   I grow elderly, alas!
Though no tittle I am losing
   Of the zeal I felt of yore,
Now and then I can't help snoozing –
   Wake me if I snore!

HARRY GRAHAM, 'LORD'S'

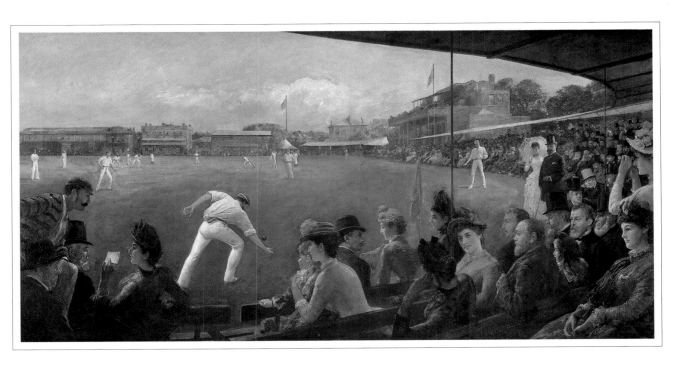

HAMPSTEAD

Hampstead indeed is risen from a little country village, to a city, not upon the credit only of the waters, 'tho 'tis apparent its growing greatness began there; but company increasing gradually, and the people liking both the place and the diversions together; it grew suddenly populous, and the concourse of people was incredible. This consequently raised the rate of lodgings, and that increased buildings, till the town grew up from a little village, to a magnitude equal to some cities; nor could the uneven surface, inconvenient for building, uncompact, and unpleasant, check the humour of the town, for even on the very steep of the hill, where there's no walking twenty yards together, without tugging up a hill, or stradling down a hill, yet 'tis all one, the buildings increased to that degree, that the town almost spreads the whole side of the hill.

Daniel Defoe, *A Tour through the Whole Island of Great Britain*, 1724–27

G.CLAUSEN. 1881

THE THAMES AT CHELSEA

The river that we know and love best – the river that sums up for us the beauty of London – lies between Waterloo Bridge and Chelsea, and the symbols of it are the barges. Up and down they drift with the tide, or lie at their moorings, broad and deep, grimy, yet beautiful in their strong curves, laden almost awash with all manner of goods; sometimes singly, oftener in strings with a noisy tugboat puffing outrageously at the head of the tow. But the tug is not doing the work; it is the river, whose laden body carries on steadfastly all these monstrous burdens, majestic in its motion, neither hasting nor resting, nor feeling the weight. That beauty – the grace of calm strength – no one can help feeling who looks at the stream, and, to gain a notion of its force, watches the race and swirl of all that weight of water round the piers. But the river is incomparable too for the mere charm of colour and line. You may see it yellow in the sun through fog, as if it really ran gold; often blue of a clear day; but oftenest of all, and still more beautiful, a silver grey, just broken, like a roughness on the metal, with flaws of wind or eddies.

STEPHEN GWYNN, *DECAY OF SENSIBILITY*

SOUTH OF THE RIVER

Opposite Chelsea on the south bank lies Battersea . . . It is generally the case in central London that the districts on the south bank of the Thames are meaner, architecturally poorer, and more heavily industrialized than those on the north bank. An historical explanation of this development is that until the first Westminster Bridge was opened in 1749, the only crossings of the Thames were by London Bridge and the ferries. The south bank was a less convenient place to live . . . The south bank was less developed until the new bridges, tunnels, and railways were built across the river in the nineteenth century. Then the industrial revolution and the Victorian terraced houses for those who worked in its factories spilled across and proliferated over the comparatively empty south bank.

Battersea is no exception to this theory. Hardly a shadow of the original village on the marshy bank of the Thames survives . . . Beside Battersea Park rise the four stately chimneys of one of the cathedrals of modern industrial architecture and one of the landmarks of the river, Battersea Power Station. White smoke seethes continuously from the smoke-stacks, which are only fifteen feet short of the cross on top of St Paul's Cathedral.

PHILIP HOWARD, *LONDON'S RIVER*, 1975

THE VIEW FROM GREENWICH HILL

We surveyed the park below us, the steep grass slope and the jagged lines of headlong trees, which seemed running post-haste downhill to join the huge leafy chestnuts on the level ground behind the Queen's House. These tilted trees and the intersecting paths beneath the hill, are the remains of an attempt at landscape gardening undertaken by Charles II on plans laid down by Le Notre. The chestnut-trees radiate outwards in irregular formation from the white box of the Queen's House, dark, billowing shapes against the lime-washed walls and the light grass. From where we stood the domed twin towers of Greenwich Hospital were scarcely outlined against the general confusion of roofs, and the chimneys across the river sent up streamers of black smoke into the toneless sky. In the middle distance was the wide reach of the river, a motionless breadth dividing Greenwich from the Isle of Dogs. There was little doing on it. The water, pallid beneath a grey-white sky, did not appear to move, and the brown-sailed rigging of an old ship passing upstream with surprising speed seemed to slide swiftly over the surface of the river like a pirates' galleon drawn across the back of a pantomime stage.

JAMES POPE-HENNESSY, *LONDON FABRIC*, 1939

THE TOWER OF LONDON

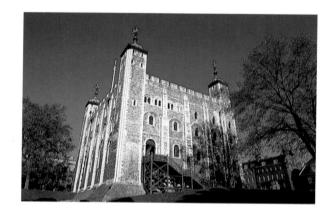

Stay yet, look back with me unto the Tower.
Pity, you ancient stones, those tender babes
Whom envy hath immured within your walls,
Rough cradle for such little pretty ones!
Rude ragged nurse, old sullen playfellow
For tender princes, use my babies well.
So foolish sorrow bids your stones farewell.

WILLIAM SHAKESPEARE, *RICHARD III*, *c*1591

BILLINGSGATE MARKET

'O ho! O ho! this way – this way – this way! Fish alive! alive! alive O!'
In the darkness of the shed, the white bellies of the turbots, strung up bow-fashion, shine like mother-of-pearl, while the lobsters, lying upon them, look intensely scarlet, from the contrast. Brown baskets piled up on one another, and with the herring-scales glittering like spangles all over them, block up the narrow paths. Men in coarse canvas jackets, and bending under huge hampers, push past, shouting 'Move on! Move on, there!' and women, with the long limp tails of cod-fish dangling from their aprons, elbow their way through the crowd . . . Little girls carrying matting-bags, that they have brought from Spitalfields, come up, and ask you in a begging voice to buy their baskets; and women with bundles of twigs for stringing herrings, cry out, 'Half-penny a bunch!' from all sides.

HENRY MAYHEW, *LONDON LABOUR AND THE LONDON POOR*, 1861

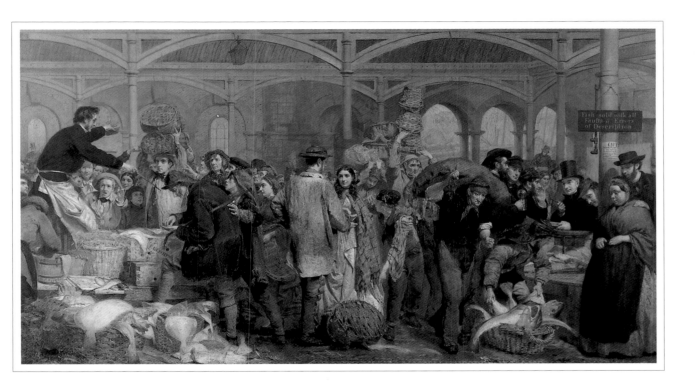

PORTOBELLO ROAD

Portobello Road on Saturdays, the best and oddest market for antiques in London, outside of the great sale-rooms and the shops of the profound specialists. To go to Portobello Road on the off days is to be treated with suspicion: Are you in the trade? Their last Queen Anne mirror went on Thursday. It is up to you whether you come again. And so on. You understand their attitude: Are you snooping around for someone? Who are you *in* with? They've never seen your face before. Are you a 'member'? You go away past the prettily done-up houses of the neighbourhood, skirt the murder area in Notting Hill Gate and pass the new housing estates and fine schools that have sprung up on the bomb sites of one of London's sinister mixed-up quarters, only half a mile from the race riots. But on Saturday you return. The Portobello inhabitants have now put on their act of being local characters, half of them out of Dickens and the other half dreamy connoisseurs. The antique trade of London is tough and intimately connected; it shows a head in innumerable districts; it is a collection of tricky eccentrics, watching one another like spies, and it is the least on-coming, the most misleadingly absent-minded trade in London.

V. S. PRITCHETT, *LONDON PERCEIVED*, 1962

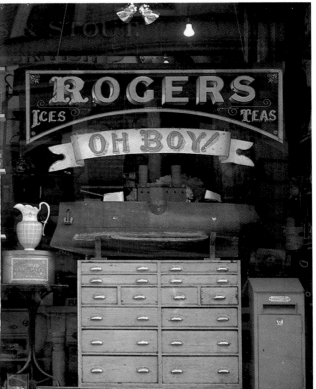

STAPLE INN

Most people know these ancient dwellings, surviving so precariously, it would seem, amid an ever renewing environment. They are the special objective of the visitor anxious to recapture something of the appearance of a past city, for they are almost the only examples left in London which help him to do so. As one looks at them and recalls some of the momentous scenes which they have witnessed, one wonders how long they will survive the ravages of time, and that beetle which is its hand-maid in the work of destruction, or the enterprising builder, who is, in this respect, almost more to be feared than either. Happily the old houses are the property of the great insurance office which, perhaps because it realizes how overwhelming are its own premises, is doing its best to preserve a more alluring type of architectural achievement. Anyhow, it is fighting that horrible insect which makes onslaught on our most cherished possessions and has no respect for tradition or for the antiquity on which it feeds.

E. Beresford Chancellor, *London Recalled*, 1937

THE LORD MAYOR'S SHOW

You cannot imagine the quantity of people there are at the windows, balconies, and in the streets to see the pageant pass. The Lord Mayor's Day is a great holiday in the City. The populace on that day is particularly insolent and rowdy, turning into lawless freedom the great liberty it enjoys. At these times it is almost dangerous for an honest man, and more particularly for a foreigner, if at all well dressed, to walk in the streets, for he runs a great risk of being insulted by the vulgar populace, which is the most cursed brood in existence. He is sure of not only being jeered at and being bespattered with mud, but as likely as not dead dogs and cats will be thrown at. him, for the mob makes a provision beforehand of these playthings, so that they may amuse themselves with them on the great day. If the stranger were to get angry, his treatment would be all the worse. The best thing to be done on these occasions is not to run the risk of mixing with the crowd; but, should you desire to do so from curiosity, you had better dress yourself as simply as possible in the English fashion, and trust to pass unnoticed.

CESAR DE SAUSSURE, LETTER, c1725

LONDON TRANSPORT

The London scene in the opening years of the century was, like the scene at the opening of the nineteenth, very much as it had been in the preceding decade. It was still a London rumbling with horse-buses, tinkling with hansoms, and shrilling with cab-whistles. Here and there an electric brougham slid noiseless through the traffic, and a few motor-cars and a stray motor-bus honked and banged, encouraged by shouts of 'Whip be'ind, guv'nor!'. . . But they were isolated in the mass of horse-traffic. This traffic was growing thicker and thicker, and on wet days the roads were a morass of mud and horse-droppings, which hoofs and wheels churned and sparked all over the pavements and shop-windows . . .

That brief Edwardian age – nine years – was for London a transition age. Old and new jostled for place. Horse-buses and motor-buses were on the roads together. Hansoms and taxis met in hate and contempt. In the year following the Coronation, the new desire for speed was recognized by the electric tram . . . But ten years were to pass before the last horse-drawn tram disappeared from the streets.

THOMAS BURKE, *THE STREETS OF LONDON*, 1940

LIGHT AND SHADE, SUN AND SMOKE

London is ugly, dusky, dreary, more destitute than any European city of graceful and decorative incident . . . London is pictorial in spite of detail – from its dark-green, misty parks, the way the light comes down leaking and filtering from its cloud-ceiling, and the softness and richness of tone, which objects put on in such an atmosphere as soon as they begin to recede. Nowhere is there such a play of light and shade, such a struggle of sun and smoke, such aerial gradations and confusions. To eyes addicted to such contemplations this is a constant diversion, and yet this is only part of it. What completes the effect of the place is its appeal to the feelings, made in so many ways, but made above all by agglomerated immensity. At any given point, London looks huge; even in narrow corners you have a sense of its hugeness, and petty places acquire a certain interest from their being parts of so mighty a whole. Nowhere else is so much human life gathered together, and nowhere does it press upon you with so many suggestions. These are not all of an exhilarating kind; far from it. But they are of every possible kind, and that is the interest of London.

HENRY JAMES, *AN ENGLISH EASTER*, 1877

ACKNOWLEDGEMENTS

PICTURE CREDITS

Front cover/23: *Piccadilly Circus*, George Hyde Pownall (Omell Gallery/Fine Art Photographs)
Back cover: *Palace of Westminster*, George Vicat Cole (Guildhall Art Gallery/Bridgeman Art Library – hereafter BAL)
Frontispiece: *St Martin in the Fields*, after William Logsdail (Gavin Graham Gallery/BAL)
3: *Heart of the Empire*, Neils Lund (Guildhall Art Gallery/BAL)
5: *Tower Bridge*, Francisco Hidelgo (Image Bank)
7: *St Mary le Strand*, George Sidney Shepherd (Private collection/BAL)
9: *Covent Garden*, Balthasar Nebot (Guildhall Art Gallery/BAL)
11: *Northumberland House and Whitehall*, Henry Pether (Museum of London)
13: *The National Gallery*, Guiseppe de Nittis (Musée du Petit Palais/Giraudon/BAL)
15: *Thames below Westminster*, Claude Monet (National Gallery, London)
17: *Towards Buckingham Palace*, John Heseltine (David Messum)
18/19: *Trooping the Colour*, Romilly Lockyer (Image Bank)
21: *Old Regent Street*, J. Kynnersley Kirby (Bradford Art Gallery/BAL)
23: *Piccadilly Circus*, George Hyde Pownall (Omell Gallery/Fine Art Photographs)
25: *Thames on a Winter's Evening*, Adam Woolfitt (Susan Griggs Agency)
26: *St. James's Park*, James Drummond (Southampton City Art Gallery)
27: *Whitehall from St James's*, Reginald Rex Vicat Cole (Fine Art Photographs)
29: *Royal Albert Hall*, Romilly Lockyer (Image Bank)
31: *Sloane Street*, Jacques Emile Blanche (City of York Art Gallery/BAL/© DACS, London 1991)
33: *England v Australia, c1886*, George Hamilton Barrable & Robert Ponsonby Staples (MCC/BAL)
35: *A Spring Morning, Haverstock Hill*, Sir George Clausen (Bury Art Gallery & Museums/BAL)
37: *View of the Thames from Chelsea Reach*, Oskar Kokoschka (Christie's/BAL/© DACS, London 1991)
39: *Albert Bridge*, John Sims
41: *View of Greenwich*, Anon. (Gavin Graham Gallery/BAL)
42: *Tower of London*, Patrick Doherty (Stockphotos)
43: *Tower of London*, Marc Romanelli (Image Bank)
45: *Billingsgate Fish Market*, George Elgar Hicks (Fishmongers Company/BAL)
46: *Portobello Market*, John Sims
47: *Portobello Market*, Adam Woolfitt (Susan Griggs Agency)
49: *Staple Inn, Holborn*, Philip Norman (Guildhall Art Gallery/BAL)
51: *Lord Mayor's Procession Arriving at the Law Courts*, Charles Cundall (Guildhall Art Gallery/BAL)
53: *A Busy Evening, Westminster Bridge*, Anon. (Fine Art Photographs)
55: *St Pancras Hotel and Station from Pentonville Road*, John O'Connor (Museum of London/BAL)

TEXT CREDITS

Text extracts from the following sources are reproduced with the kind permission of the publishers and copyright holders stated. Should any copyright holder have been inadvertently omitted they should apply to the publishers who will be pleased to credit them in full in any subsequent editions.

4, 14, 46: V. S. Pritchett, *London Perceived* (Chatto & Windus, 1962); 18: Rex Alston, *Flower of Cities* (Max Parrish, 1949); 22: Noël Coward, London at Night' from *After the Ball* (Chappell Music Ltd, 1954); 28: Priscilla Metcalf, *Victorian London* (Cassell 1972); 38: Philip Howard, *London's River* (Hamish Hamilton, 1975); 40: James Pope-Hennessy, *London Fabric* (Batsford, 1939); 48: E. Beresford Chancellor, *London Recalled* (Basil Blackwell, 1937); 52: Thomas Burke, *The Streets of London* (Batsford, 1940).

First U.S. Edition

ISBN 1-55970-161-7

Library of Congress Catalog Card Number 91-55227
Library of Congress Cataloging-in-Publication information
is available.

Published in the United States by Arcade Publishing, Inc.,
New York, a Little, Brown company

10   9   8   7   6   5   4   3   2   1

Conceived, edited and designed by Russell Ash & Bernard Higton
Text research by Steve Dobell
Picture research by Mary-Jane Gibson

Printed in Spain